SONGS OF A RETURNING SOUL

Books by Elizabeth Libbey

The Crowd Inside
Songs of a Returning Soul

SONGS OF A RETURNING SOUL

ELIZABETH LIBBEY

POEMS

Carnegie-Mellon University Press
Pittsburgh 1981

Feffer and Simons Inc., London

Acknowledgments

Some of these poems first appeared in the following
publications to whose editors grateful acknowledgment
is made for permission to reprint:

Ascent: "Juana Bautista Lucero, Circa 1926, To her
Photographer"; *Barat Review:* "Practicing Parts," "The
Woman of Two Groves"; *Canto:* "To the Naked Couple
Downstairs," "The Continuing History"; *Ironwood:*
"Whiteout: An Entry From the Journal of Milton
Walworth Ensign, Montana Winter of 1879"; *Ploughshares:*
"Juncture"; *Poetry:* "Deja Vú," "Girl Sitting Alone in
Her Room," "Late One Night," "Apparent Horizon,"
"Themselves".

The publication of this book is supported by grants
from the National Endowment for the Arts in Washington,
D.C., a Federal agency, and from the Pennsylvania
Council on the Arts.

CONTENTS

IV

V

* * *

for my brother, Bill
> *"I should go with him in the bloom,*
> *Hoping it might be so."*

— from "The Oxen," Thomas Hardy

SONG OF THE SECOUDDI TRIBE

for Niall Boggs

Little one, we tell
on the singing logs of the feast
before the rains, the celebration
of our souls returning
through the tops of the trees.
We invite our souls
which have travelled far from us,
to visit. We carve these pleasing birds
from the heart of the banana tree,
we let them wear the feathers,
the brave ornaments of our fathers,
we hang each bird before a doorway
in the wind where our souls can see.
We dance all night in the fire,
pass from the days of carelessness
into the day of compassion given
by the fathers.

Little one, you must
come again to us, you must come
in a year and again in a year and again
and together we will drive
bad spirits from the tribal home,
we will sacrifice the pig
and eat, we
will beg his forgiveness, we will sing
to his soul. Sit, we will sing
the song of the blackbird
as he flies from the top
of the oldest tree at the top of the sacred
mountain. We will paint our faces
the face of the blackbird, the color
of the root and the blood.

Little one, you
must travel now beneath the trees
of your fathers, you must put on
the ancient bones. Take up
now the power of the song, rise

and go to the door of your house.
Open it. You must let
the wings enter in,
and you will be happy perhaps,
as you are today,
held in the arms of your mother
as she stands in the river
which is clean and strong, and bids you listen
to the river song your father sings.

I

NARCISSUS TWILIGHT

Having spent all day hollowing out my bones,
thinking I hear every dog's bark
rise into a scream just behind my shoulder blade,
I come home, force myself
into a chair, force again this discipline,
the one patience
articulate of love, care, this dance I do
to keep myself from taking things apart
I can't make whole. Positioning
in a thought, what the spine knows: there's no
letting go. Making the dance push against
the soft shell of the skull, I keep
this vigil: suppose
the usual sparrow idling at my window,
sudden in some fascination, crushes
feathers and beak against glass. I watch
it smear itself across the image of my face.
Even so, my hands must stay
crushed against my knees, and spine hold
though it cracks. The architecture
of patience must hold.
I say to myself, I love you, love you, be still,
pretending a twilight I never feel.
At dawn I will sleep, my body an afterthought
night leaves on the sheets. I'll wake,
already raw, to walls' blue serenity,
with beak and lost eye
still to be dusted from the sill.
I would hold you, hold you. Be still. Be
careful, what I care for
no longer has the power to please. Not even
Elizabeth, Elizabeth.
I sit, I go out and come back
in every subtlety of light. And no matter what
I must wait for that transformation
of light to dark, that breaking up
when the names of things are finally lost in the blood.

CELEBRATION AT ZENO'S OYSTER BAR

The man she's just met asks
where she lives. She names
a suburb, how
unusually warm the winter there.
Behind her, two
angel-fish lock jaws, crash
through to air. Scales
torn free, float
directionless, poise in the arms
of miniature aquarium trees.

She dips among heaped platters
of crawfish, oysters,
her fingers suddenly careless
of heads, eyes, claws crushed damp
against her palms. She names
the exact distance between home and work, two
miles work to home, and how
long in good weather, bad, but he
stares, this man, so long so straight
into her words, it's clear he sees

she's the arrow in flight
dividing distance on itself
until it seems she's never moved
beyond her words, that her hand
isn't floating now toward his
across this ruined feast,
that she's
only a fine-honed politeness
designed to please a stranger.

THE CONTINUING HISTORY

He tells me the Mississippi
is rising, the only thing between
us and disaster
is this levee we're parked on watching
the wet lights of barges slide
heavily into fog. Leaning back, I remember
the story of Louisiana turtles—they too
distrust rising tides
that undercut the levee, and eddies
grown dangerous as snags
in the river at night. Those turtles simply climb
out of the water and walk to town.

Pulling my jeans back up
over my hips, I say nothing. His hand searches
for mine on the dark front seat, but I've
pulled it up into my silk sleeve.
I've backed casually against the door
and sunk my head into my shoulders.
Someday He'll thank me for undoing
his faith in World War II movies
where the sailor tricks the girl
with, "Tomorrow
I'm being shipped out, and who knows?"
but leter, patriotic, he longs
for a wife, a house in the country.
He longs to make of her an honest woman.

I suggest a dinner
of raw fish and jazz at the hottest spot
in town. Tonight in my room alone,
I'll pull down my jeans and survey
with pleasure, my awakened nerves, the rosy skin
along my thighs. I'll search my bookshelves
for a way to frame this: not
the prince or toad, not maiden waked
from long sleep. But the tortoise and hare, or how
the industrious ant prepared
for winter while the romantic grasshopper sang
and sang with his long legs stuck out into the Autumn air
while the river rose, snow began, the world
slid into history, yes, the turtle
moving through, carrying itself underneath
its casual back.

TO THE NAKED COUPLE DOWNSTAIRS

for Leslie Ullman

And it is not a matter of place:
wherever I am, I'm always
the woman upstairs.
I lie robed on my bed, my
cheek against the wall. I keep
my arms at my sides, my knees locked
under the sheet. No matter what.

Or I rise
for wine and little cakes.
As I sip, I walk
into and out of each room, thinking
to keep it dark. I try
to erase my bare feet on the rugs,
the animal rasp crumbs
make against my lips.
I try to erase my breath
which is always taking up space.

One night not long ago,
I was wild with silence. My voice
moaned where the wall touched my skin.
I loosened my robe, twisted
into the sheets, hoping you might
notice. But your silence
only pushed up harder against the floor.
I was up all night. I drank, ate
nothing. Once I imagined
I slammed the door.

Tonight I'm myself again.
Slowly, slowly I turn in my bed,
smoothing the wrinkles out as I go.
I wait for your silence
to work through my mattress, through the sore
skin of my back. Sometimes
I feel nighttime
work itself into a scream. That
is your night, not mine.

THE OPENING OF THE LANDSCAPE

Somewhere close to her
it is evening, green fading.
Voices slip from their hiding places.

Standing on the porch, she senses
the bunching of muscles,
the gathering herself close along the ground,
and as she does, the animals
begin to gather beside her, encircle her
under the red moon. Their loud hearts
disturb the dusk, their delicate lashes
wash back and forth across her eyes.

Belly low in dry grass, she stalks
the lighted house that twinkles far off
as if it were not where she lives,
drawing the curtains each evening, dusk being
a stare she can't afford to return.

From the porch, she listens
to the moon slide in among grasses,
close enough to embrace.
Nothing now but moist air on her lips,
and a dry moon rustling
animal backs, the crackle of water on tongues.

Somewhere, distant as planets, animals
pad round and round an invisible water
on another invisible night.

II

DEJA VÚ

From the mulberry limb, I stared down
into my brother's face
as if, gazing at water expecting myself, I gazed
on someone else.
"Jump," he offers, arms rising toward me
like the arms of one drowning.
But how could I, slung motionless, thin-aired,
trying to lower myself by eye
a leaf at a time, a house floor by floor,
be a purple splash of grackles attacking the lawn,
save him, I
who don't jump, but ride
the slight swell of breeze forever?
"Jump," I breathe, as the mulberry carries me off, my
arms falling toward my brother like water
closing over.

FLOWN CARDINAL

Father points. He makes the sound
again, high in his throat. "No other
bird sings that song, you know," he says,
bending close to my ear. I hold
my breath to hear, press close
to the glass, peering into splash of evergreen,
3rd branch up, right side, near
patch of sky, but my eyes
can't hold red of beak or wing, brushing of green
bough against feather breast. Only wind.

"There, he's
flicking his tail, do you see?"
"Yes," I lie, my eyes skittering
from sky to tree to ground, my
voice disappearing inside
Father's face reflected in the window. Watching
me. And I do
see—the rustle of Father's hand knotting
inside his pocket as he
turns from the window, the bright
flash just going out in his eyes.

PRACTICING PARTS

When the grownups bring my brother home
from the ballgame, thumb broken
from a desperate slide into home,
I'm caught standing on the stairs
in Mother's lavender travelling dress,
Grandmother's gauzy red scarf. Two
mounds of kleenex stuffed
down against my narrow chest.

Father carries my brother, trailing hero's dust,
to the couch. I descend clattering
in Mother's spike heels. I've awaited
his return, felt there's a war
going on close by, and now kneeling beside him,
kleenex settling around my waist,
everything fits me perfectly
as if I've waited always for this moment,
gripping his good hand
in mine, weeping because my brother
in his baseball suit and sweat, purple heart,
will not.

Pulling the kleenex out
from under Mother's dress, I wipe
the sweat from his neck, kiss the thick tape
wrapped around his thumb. . . . Brother, we
are perfect at this moment: we are what
we are supposed to be.

LATE ONE NIGHT

for Ida Elizabeth Boggs

My mother's voice rises when she says
the world has changed, even snow
falls without value or taste.
What was wonderland, she says, is tracked through.
I think she's reminded of grown children
who arrive for holidays, wearing
the tracks of their lives on their faces.
What, bending over the cradle, no mother
ever sees. My mother saw a skin
so translucent she could believe
the world new, for the world she suspected
was still unlit there. Now
I sit before her, thirty-two.

So tonight my mother refuses the world,
remembers herself the child
who listens in predawn light for the horse
the color of milk, clopping its way
up the cobbled street. Its hooves kick
snow back against the wheels, milk bottles clatter
deep in the wagon, and the driver in white
adjusts his cap for first sun, calls good morning
to the windows of houses he knows by heart,
his horse dancing its head side
to side to say all's well, and never
breaks gait, knowing the route blind.

By snowlight we watch, on the deep
white roofs of neighbors, those insensible marks
of bird or wind or fir bough
disappear. My mother listens, head cocked,
for hooves, someone
riding all night for love. Wind
is all, wind blows the tracks away.
We sit across the table from each other
until enough snow has fallen.

MEMORY: SHOULD YOU PICK IT UP?

Cricket-voice caught in
tight mesh of window screen. Again,
the invitation: begin, let
memory come apart
like movie machines. Put to the test: fray, spark,
disconnect. Walk out
to the dark, all the pasts
of crickets dropping at your feet.

Why, whenever green acorns bounce
on the hoods of cars by streetlight, hollow-slap,
do you start? do you say 'too soon, too
soon?' Calm. Begin
now when leaves . . . feel how they turn
luminous around you as the sap drops back?
Vein-empty: so, to start
with nothing to sustain. What was it
that seemed most you this morning?

You find simply a Here, hear
your voice rustle at your shoulder, wanting
in and out, in, out. Whatever
of desire, the invitation is this night,
these particular crickets. These
acorns bouncing irreverant
under the moon . . . as they drop to the street,
in you also their caps jar
from their heads, their green fills you
as no other greenness could.

You walk out as if never before
have you, recognizing nothing. But what
is there to know so much?
Now in this night you raise your head
as from a sleep. That disc emptying
its hard light into your face: wasn't it
once all you looked up to? Let
fall, let fall the helmet, the skin

of all you believe
or remember or thought you remembered.

And love? A rustling, leaves fluttering
against your chest, hollow-slap. Leaves
blown free . . . nodding
off again? You aren't looking for, but
here is: spark, ignite,
the irreverant heart. Crickety-Heart drowning
out its name. And your dishevelled
bones? How came they here at your feet? Poke
yourself to see, just
to see once and for all. What was it
you dreamed, what did you want to say? Whatever
of desire, begin again. Let be. Walk
into just to see. To see once and for all.

III

SABBATH, JANUARY 25, 1981

This is the year of our lord, lady—
a brilliant day, all
the golden innocence returned
to those who've mislayed.
Don't peek out so with those eyes,
those sorry lashes. Remember,
in the beginning is rumor
of wings in a thankless universe,
and his whispered litany, "lift me."
Enfolded, you lie
watching the light grow sad where it touches
his forearms. You stare
past him into the sky: air isn't angry,
you are happy to lie
beneath air, your real lover.
To touch that cloudy face would be to shatter.

On this brilliant day, our lady
of crows, of fallen flocks and still waters,
you walk around the block and wave to neighbors,
belly indiscreet beneath your shawl.
Sun turns your skin honey and salt,
ashes, bread—what he
takes gladly in his mouth always once more.
No Hereafter above you
where stiff-necked you must hope to arrive,
not even a Here-and-Now where you must play
coy mistress to some death or other.
Nobody's instrument, the stars
are too far, too far apart
to mass an attack out of night's kindness. Perhaps
this twilight or the next, one random
star wild with heat will impact. One random parting
smile from you might send
the moment on its way, and who recall?

Man and woman, man-of-the-womb, back home
beside you, he watches
the sparrow on the sill peck where he
has placed dried fruit and seed.
You watch him watch the sparrow hop

in and out of his reflection in the glass.
In the beginning is explosion wild
with matter, a million wings rise off
black water, and everything born.
You are part of this long line
of particles' concern. A culmination
seated in your chair, watching
the music of faith, music of the starved heart
as it goes round and round on the phonograph.
He lights the lamp and passes,
brushing your cheek with the back of his hand.
You embrace his waist, kiss the cloth
where it covers his ribs, as you have
a thousand times. Litany
of marriage. And as he goes, you notice
for the first time the doorway
rises up to embrace his passing. A day
when what is mislayed
is returned. A brilliant day. It is not
what you wanted, remember? You wanted

to desire nothing at all.
But it returns the air to you: weapons dissolve,
your wrist heals, air heals around you
where you sit. Innocence
returned: the unborn
shifts, the breath
of an untried lover drifts in your hair.
You, lost beside him always, dream your dream
of accomplished escapes, conjuring
the beak that drives into your wrist
again and again that you might bear some pain.
But today, were you to ask,
air could seduce your palm. At least
it seems so—he in another room, humming
winged and free. The year of, lady, like any other—
to touch that face would be
to shatter it. As in the beginning,
how many times you will.

GIRL SITTING ALONE IN HER ROOM

Her book unopened rests.

A single dolphin breaks surface.
What has always been
grey ocean is suddenly ivory, iron
strands of shadow across a back arched
green, fin glistening
in green spray shot with violet when spray hits sun
midair, eye's black eclipse disappearing
amid fringes, swirls lingering,
surface erupts again molten silver into gold
gasp of air, release.

Mother stands carefully in the doorway
looking around. Is
everything in order?

The girl sits at dinner,
watching her plate.

Back in her room, everything is
in order: curtains sway, a single spider
crosses the ceiling, lets down
its thin strand. Water
rolls, subsides, sun
settles on bottom coral, dolphin
amid slants of light dancing, rocking
on its tail. Black
eyes waiting.

THE WOMAN OF TWO GROVES

I walk out from the others
at dusk to the orchard
and plucking a calabash, already fallen, from the grass,
I tuck it against my breasts.
I'll walk back looking like I've found
love out there, and sitting away
from the fire-talk, I'll fashion fruit to gourd.
Come morning when I dip water from the urn,
I'll taste it new, tinged with remembrance
of hot winds, white sun, while everything human
sleeps close to the cooling circle of stones.
I'll forget the distant pomegranate's
silhouette each dusk
when I strolled to my lover's bed.
I'll tire of sharp resonance from another life—
crimson pulp against my teeth, seed
spilling across my tongue.

JUANA BAUTISTA LUCERO, CIRCA 1926, TO HER PHOTOGRAPHER

I open up, mop gray ice
from the counter with my sleeve.
Place the pickles and eggs carefully before me.
December so suddenly: harsh
shadow, white sun. I, ninety-two
long as I remember.
And I unlock my door each morning
as if it were nothing. I watch
shadows against the door, how when wind comes,
they slide across the floor and up the counter
to my arm, how they curl into my palm
and when I turn there they are sprawled
along the wall. From this I know
all things pass through me.

The town comes to buy what I won't sell—
floursack apron on its peg, my
spotted hand. They want to have
something. A memento. They mistake me
for a man the way my nose has curled
under and my face darkened, but I'm more
legible with each sun, head sunk
into my thick neck. I wear
nothing that is mine. It is all
only a shadow caught in my head.

Mornings, I set my mirror
against the wrinkled window-glass and let
the sun dance however it will.
Evenings I turn that mirror on myself, bring
it close because I am no fool:
I am alive today for you. I fix
my hair, tie your bright scarf about my neck.
You want to hold a shadow, want the light
harsh and darkness filling up my eyes.
When I am frozen in myself, won't I grow
younger? Won't they look at me
a hundred years from here and know, was I
a woman or a man? Pick
the mirror up from the sill, and look and set
it down again. Let it, like any window,
have what it wants of dust.

IV

OFFERING TO A STRANGER

What your back is, is that you?
You stand so straight at
the window, what
do you wait for, and where do
your arms go, the hands, does their
intent rest in my own, might I
try your fist on, your caress?

What have I, after all, to say?
The lines of my face
deepen in your back, and still
you don't turn. Would you, if
I parted my lips and spoke, take
from them this sound and own
it yours, own to
a gentleness, gentle
as the way your coat sags at
your stiff shoulders?

A stranger in a coat
before a window—what can
it mean to me? Still, your arguments
go out into the day. Might not
these arguments be
an offering to say, She who betrays
the air and stands behind you
incessantly breathing,
coat fallen, is forgiven?

APPARENT HORIZON

We sit together in a room, you a landscape
talking calmly of snow. Me remembering
in snow shadows drifting across the blue walls,
that everything comes apart up close
and is again resolved only by the eye.
Take you, for instance, what snow shadows do
to your face, it
line by line forgets itself, disperses
into this room's blue spaces, making my hand
open despite its love of fist,
the fingers uncurling one by one
across blank surfaces of air toward
the arc of your jaw. We're
the possibility of horizon, for
in blue air aren't we
the earth returned
perpetually to itself, juncture the eye finds
again, again, and aren't
we the range of each other?
                              Understand
I mean finally to touch your face, to watch
it take shape again under
hand's perception of skin—a resolution
like to the eye's, not our lives
rushing close, caressed
by brevity—cloud, shadow of cloud, and
if I understand
nothing, still this delight
that we're transformed, sifted
through each other even as we sit talking
in snow shadows drifting, our ghosts floating free.
In this way, we
are already the picture remembered later: how
my hand rose and set along the curve
of your face, how we briefly
caressed the world with ourselves, the only
way we knew, even as our eyes
restore us to our landscape sharp
beside a window in a room one afternoon, looking
out for ourselves.

UNDER CLOUD

for Barry Spacks

They walk, they take the air.
Her plain breasts excite against
exotic purple all the way
from India. If it rained
now, if just one cloud
lowered and opened its blessings out,
purple suggestion
would catch in her arms' fine hair,
purple smear across her cheek
where she has brushed
her hair back with her sleeve.

He turns his fine brown
eye on her, "ah, dolphins," he says,
laughs, and she "no,
birds," her breasts skim just under
purple sea, the season
dropping softly all around.

Beneath his tunic, midnight
blue, she knows are birds restless
in a starless sky, and dolphins
inflaming surfaces. It's easy,
she thinks, to see his shirt is wise
the way he wears it, wise against rain,
and not asking for trouble
from the air. But once when he
didn't know she saw, he was dangerous
in black silk inlaid
with fins and wings, he conjured any
clouds he pleased, all the while practicing
the sound, the right sound of speech:

if it should rain. If
it should rain, the skin
will suffer nothing. The heart
is so easily covered.
Ah, revolutionary heart,
planning once more its big breakout.

THEMSELVES

He reads, curling uncurling his hand.
He is not thinking of her,
though thinking of space, all times, about air,
he reads her. She
walks room to room, surveying
corners, how they expand
into closets of heaped belongings
not in their places the minute her back is turned.

Standing at the edge of shadow and light,
she watches his reading, each
finger, each tendon, as if he heard a music.
She rearranges
her delicate hair, steps back
into the shadowed kitchen to practice
standing outside his hand,
and for the first time in a long time she hears
the wind like closing thunder against the door,
the shadows draw her farther in.

He has turned the page: the scene
is a woman of many longings reading him
from the shadows. And he thinks, There is always
room for one more darkness, one less light
to think about, one less stunned window
stuck in its frame. And he thinks, If she
were to move that movement would be
the word he wondered at this morning, but could
not find: animals padding, padding
away. Look
up now, says the scene, and he does, up
into the room, up through the air.
Darkness everywhere. She has put
the rooms to bed one by one for the night.

V

WHITEOUT: AN ENTRY FROM THE JOURNAL OF MILTON WALWORTH ENSIGN, MONTANA WINTER OF 1879.

Monday: snow. I move my hand
through the cold, margin to margin,
not to fill up whiteness, step in it
like stunned deer, but to bend
this interminable thin blue line
over on itself into letters into words into—
architectures, arcs that curve
back on themselves into weeks into years into—Ensign
writing amid all-whirling blizzard
of one fine point: buffalo
where they faithfully hold the horizon,
stumble along it, hoar-white, nostrils jammed with ice.

I think: Ensign
seated on his steamer trunk stares out
through frenzied tent-flap at blizzard and through it
to buffalo. He records what he sees, records
himself seeing, curves it until it crosses
a familiar ground. But what? Ensign?
Ensign, as the collapsible mapmaker's table
collapses, scattering
railroad charts, account books, red
signal lantern across the frozen-open ground.

Snow. Monday. Continuous. Ensign
sleeps without North, without sky, with no star
bending to him. He notes down
without pen, with no paper, no ink, the presence
of someone's breath nearby. But who? Ensign?
Journal tucked close to his ribs he sees
himself discovered years later
by this great faithful breath, by a new generation
of eyelids heavy with ice. He remembers
at the last to fix his hand in place—designing tool
for the blue line he would pull
through endless possibilities of snow.

And if he is right, I am right.
He has closed the journal, nodded off, but I

have not finished:
                         Monday: snow. The buffalo
bend in thin line back on themselves, huddle,
accepting the offer of a moment's rest
from what hasn't happened. I move my hand
through the cold. That breath out there grazing
the railbed, working red glass into its tongue,
navigating by some peculiar instinct, enters,
stretches out in my chest. Looking down
at my hand, I read, "I wonder how much
will last," I nod, and my hands
turn palm up open now, take in
the interminable blue line. Letters curve,
swell through my palms, up my arms.
Behind my eyes: Ensign. Buffalo. Unseen
possibility of horizon
rounded to winter's closed hand.

THINKING INTO BIRDS

for Marion William Boggs

"Je veulx changer mes pensers en oyseaux,
Mes doux souspirs en zephyres nouveaux,
Qui par le monde evanteront ma pleinte."
                    —Pierre deRonsard

I. Rockville, Md., December 1980.

Father. First light begins first
with him. I stand at the window watching
him pass through my reflection and beyond
in his great maroon Hudson's Bay
mackinaw into the yard. He dips gloved hands
into the sack: millet, oak seed, pistachio, sun-
flower, thistle fly out across the air.
His breath rises up over his shoulder
as he bends to break the ice-skin
on the birdbath.
                    I can't see his face
but know in the slow-motion way he moves
he's aware without looking up of the pine
boughs filling with jay, junco,
cardinal, mourning dove, fox-
sparrow in beginning snow. How is it
they know him? his coat, his sharp eyes?

I put my mouth against the glass, kiss
out to the back of his head just as he
looses the last handful of seed
falling at the edge of the woods among
Fall's leaves. He turns to wave
though now sun strikes the window glaring
so he can't see me waving. At his back
juncos already are rattling the leaves.

II. From the Journal of M.W. Boggs,
    U.S. Navy: London, Nov. 1944.

Step out,
after 60/40 sausage, brussel sprouts, tea,
into red glow of Russell Square direct hit,
crowd murmuring. Holiday
gaiety, I'll say when I write her.

Straighten cap, straighten shoulders. Lucky
to be here among the British and their Bulldog
on this beautiful night, stars and scattered clouds.
Clear night for piloted bombers.

In Chicago, America, U.S.A., Ida
plants begonias in the window box:
reds, whites. But, she writes, there's no
blue begonia.

I am proud to strike a blow for freedom,
liberty. Her in Chicago.
These crowds go on like nothing's happened,
as if no block has disappeared. Two figures wave
from the old Russell Hotel, one side open
bed-linen and all to the night air.
Nothing out of the ordinary. Carry on,
righto, there's a good chap.

Behind blackout curtains, candles
being lit. The air-raid warden yells to get
that curtain *all the way* closed.

They say
a moving target is harder to hit, so walk
fast, faster, don't run though late for the flick,
finally a good one, Gary Cooper, "For Whom
the Bell Tolls". Friends wondering
in lobby what. The possibility of being. The odds
are in the moving target's favor, odds are with

U.S. Navy, 2nd Lt., j.g., Boggs, M.W.
of Mexico, Missouri.

You only hear the V-2s coming after they explode.
Air whistling ashes, eyes swell and tear.
Ashes that drop on the shoulders must be brushed off
immediately or they will work their way into the fabric.
Gaiety, I'll write her, of ashes children catch
on their tongues, like they might catch snow in Chicago.

Full house, friends all present and accounted for.
In the aisle, red light for alert, green light
for all clear. Gary Cooper appears
at the bridge, craters close on Westminster,
Tower of London refusing to fall.
The bridge blows up on screen, AA guns out on
the street: red light alert. Nobody moves
from his seat.

What do they do with those wing-clipped Ravens that keep
Britain free? They must just go on pecking
the manicured Tower lawns.

In Chicago, Ida sits on the window seat, towel
draped over her shoulder. She holds Boggs, Charles William,
11 months yesterday.

>Dear Son,
>>I am he returned from long ago, who shall
>>be known to you from this day forward
>>as Father.

>Dear Son,
>>All the king's horses and all the king's men
>>couldn't. All the king's cellars
>>are bomb shelters filled with angry shelves
>>of Bourdeaux, Mosel, Napolean Brandy.

Step out into quiet blackout, fog has moved in. Not knowing
which way to walk, walk, keep walking until something

makes you stop. Tomorrow, a package from Mexico, Missouri:
6 bars dark chocolate, 1 pair dark socks. And tomorrow
a letter and photo from Chicago.

"I want," I'll write her. Yes, the red leather book I picked
from Russell Square Library's rubble. Sheer chance it
wasn't burned. I'll say, *"Mon cuoeur en feu."* You only
hear them coming after.

III. Colter Bay, Wyoming, June 1966.

Father puts his glasses aside and settles
back against roots of the Ponderosa
at bay's edge. He closes his eyes and folds
his hands together. I snap the picture; thrushes explode
out of the thicket behind him, their shadows
sweeping across his face. The bay breeze stirs
leaf, moss, needle; sun trembles
on his khaki shirt as he breathes. The still-
life revising itself with each
minute shift of sun. I put

the camera aside and look away: bay, wild
onion, mint, ice-age boulders interspersed
with stands of peeling aspen, blue
shadows of spruce and behind them mountain,
low cloud and one ragged passage of birds.
If my father looked up now, he'd know them by
backsweep of wing or suggestion of formation.
Some half-completed cry. I snap
a study in texture: orderly rows of waves
that dissolve against his boot-heels. I put

the camera aside. Eyes still closed, one hand
moves from his chest, caresses
air's surfaces. I do not take the picture of my father
asleep, and in love with the air.
Tanager and Purple Martin. Teewit, Titmouse, Wren.
Loon and Copper Trogan. Philomela, Phoenix rising,
Icarus' failed wings. All birds

43

in flight, I've read, mediate between
us and heaven. My hands
in sleep, sometimes, reach out
to brush the surprised shadows
of thrushes from his eyes.

Eyes still closed, my father says,
"to think I never had a picture of you then. In London.
That you weren't in the world till later."
Were he to snap a picture of me now,
it would show a face stoic as his own,
and behind that, beak,
wing, dark eye, trying to come together
in midair. And behind,
how sun moves always revising; how sudden
branches strike through the sun.

JUNCTURE

for Neil Lukatch

Seated in the dark, my elbows propped
on the kitchen table, I can't clearly recollect
you who move inside me like water within motion,
though I choose you over and over with care,
and though my notion of air
beats in my temples as if I've gone
through your heart to get to it.

Touchable, we
must be taken and held, taken and released.
Vanishing, I always mean
to embrace, always I mean my nest of skin
to be air's fine taste.

Here, no light
to hold the curves of our skin,
yet we take shape inside
all the shapes that dark promises.

Elbows propped across from mine,
cigarette brightening
as you breathe in, you say nothing, making me want
to speak something grand for the sake of language,
but it is your breath
which so changes me, floating out
against the tips of my out-stretched fingers.

Breathing together as night
breaks up among tree limbs, and the blades
of roofs are bared, we recede
while we sit, recede to resume
the firm shape of our lives.

I can't skim your face, offer it back
as if I understood
it bottomless, teeming. You are no
comfortable kind of vision. But you've done
what you never promised: appeared
at the center of this dark I call mine,
as if irrevocable distances of mind
can fuse, and the houses of our lives join.

A RIDDLE IN HONOR OF THE NEW YEAR

for Harry Hild

"Dead in dead light," I said
one winter night as we sat side by side in a bar.
You stared into your beer, thinking
the statement from every angle until its certainty
was clear: this is to become of us, arms
laid out flesh to flesh atop the damp
mahogony bar. I wasn't thinking then of snow,
but of air tearing open and mountains
asserting themselves in the mirror before our faces.
I imagined our skulls opening
like the dome of a building sliding away.

Tonight, the year has passed. Standing
together in the yard, we pass whiskey back and forth
between us. What we don't think to say
is said for us this winter night
closing in around, hurrying snow dissolving
the dark, all permanence of form.
I spread my hand against your philosophic beard
and think of distance: perhaps only
those hidden stars are important, those wise
concentrations of light, even
if it's their ghosts we see, their afterlife.

Sometimes standing at a window I dream
vague certainties: that I might memorize
the catalogue of things: what a window is, or a wind,
and how they revise the branches of trees.
But the language I know is this night: ambiguity
of solid dark dissolving into broken white.
You, adrift, head tilted up
against a snow or any other falling.
But what will mediate
against this sudden drama of firecrackers, bells?
Remember the riddle in the old movie: what is it

always and never new, what is the difference
between the thistle and the kiss? asks the ghost.

"Transience," you smile, "needs a thought so great
it could pull the gods down." Not even
our shadows hold us long, yet they
are the root of my imagining. Shadows filling
up with snow or sun. Nights like this
are the beginning, the long slow
letting ourselves out. What I want is what I've always feared
of loving: roots pulling free, the torn place the earth
leaves in the universe as it goes. Snow
disappearing where
it touches the warmth of the hand.

* * *

PSYCHE AT THE GRAVESIDE

Sometimes my wings were hands like his
when we joined. My wild
song stilled, my wings sought the dark
calm of his pockets, longing
to live there curled, to dream of flying
out only as far as might his arms
from his sides. But I dreamed

awake all night he caught me up
and buried my wings in the dirt.
"This is your sky," he urged me, over
and over like prayer. Looking
into his hands, he nodded, "Yes,
a man's not meant to fly, this now
is your sky," and packed
the dirt down hard against my crumpled wings.

When did his smooth glass face shatter,
and that ancient city he loved
collapse in him? He was tall as a tower,
built on himself, climbing up
through himself. Though his hands
began to lose the feel
for stone on stone, though his pockets
were always filling with dirt,
he could still turn out the light, shut
his eyes and I was there covering
his hands with fine down.

"This," he mused, "is your sky," as he
pressed himself to the earth
to hide the fine down of his arms.
To choose the earth is to shelter
in a house where walls nail
themselves to the skin, and ceiling
closes over, is to finally
remember the feel for stone. I bore
universe to him. Why can't I

find in this husk of him a heart
to carry off with me?

And so I come here like a dusk
to lie beside him. A wind
flutes the seams of my wings,
and trees on the edge of my eye
seed the failed light with leaves.
His eyes say nothing staring up
past my going.

Carnegie-Mellon Poetry

1975
The Living and the Dead, Ann Hayes
In the Face of Descent, T. Alan Broughton

1976
The Week the Dirigible Came, Jay Meek
Full of Lust and Good Usage, Stephen Dunn

1977
*How I Escaped from the Labyrinth and
    Other Poems*, Philip Dacey
The Lady from the Dark Green Hills, Jim Hall
For Luck: Poems 1962-1977, H.L. Van Brunt
By the Wreckmaster's Cottage, Paula Rankin

1978
New & Selected Poems, James Bertolino
The Sun Fetcher, Michael Dennis Browne
A Circus of Needs, Stephen Dunn
The Crowd Inside, Elizabeth Libbey

1979
Paying Back the Sea, Philip Dow
Swimmer in the Rain, Robert Wallace
Far From Home, T. Alan Broughton
The Room Where Summer Ends, Peter Cooley
No Ordinary World, Mekeel McBride

1980
*And the Man Who Was Traveling Never Got
    Home*, H.L. Van Brunt
Drawing on the Walls, Jay Meek
The Yellow House on the Corner, Rita Dove
The 8-Step Grapevine, Dara Wier
The Mating Reflex, Jim Hall

1981
A Little Faith, John Skoyles
Augers, Paula Rankin
Walking Home from the Icehouse, Vern Rutsala
Work and Love, Stephen Dunn
The Rote Walker, Mark Jarman
Morocco Journal, Richard Harteis
Songs of a Returning Soul, Elizabeth Libbey

DATE DUE

GAYLORD

PRINTED IN U.S.A.